OPRAH

40 INSPIRATIONAL LIFE LESSONS AND POWERFUL WISDOM FROM OPRAH WINFREY

ENTREPRENEUR PUBLISHING

COPYRIGHT

DISCLAIMER

Your Free Gift

As a special Thank You for downloading this book I have put together an exclusive report on Morning Habits.

Learn how to build your own morning routine to achieve increased productivity and less stress. Includes sample morning routines and exclusive tips towards creating your own.

>> You Can Download This Free Report By Clicking Here <<

Kindle 5 Star Books

Free Kindle 5 Star Book Club Membership

Join Other Kindle 5 Star Members Who Are Getting Private
Access To Weekly Free Kindle Book Promotions

Get free Kindle books

Stay connected:

Join our Facebook group

Follow Kindle 5 Star on Twitter

Also, if you want to receive updates on Entrepreneur
Publishing's new books, free promotions and Kindle
countdown deals sign up to their New Release Mailing List.

For entrepreneurs: http://www.entrepreneurfinesse.com

TABLE OF CONTENTS

INTRODUCTION

Oprah Winfrey is much more than a talk show host or television personality. Oprah was listed as the most influential woman in her generation and according to Forbes magazine, she is the richest African American and the world's only Black billionaire. Oprah started life from humble beginnings as the child of a young single mother. After moving from rural Mississippi to live with her father, Oprah began to explore the possibilities of working in television. She began co-anchoring the evening news locally while she was still in her teens. However, Oprah was prone to emotional ad-libbing, which prompted her transfer to a daytime talk show. The Oprah Winfrey Show was established in 1986 and Oprah maintained that her show would be kept free of exploitative and trashy tabloid topics. While this hurt her initial ratings, viewer respect grew and the show experienced a major upsurge in popularity, allowing the show to air for twenty-five years until 2011.

Oprah has used this influence to raise awareness for charitable programs, earning her the title of greatest Black philanthropist from Business Week in 2005. Oprah established the Angel Network, which has risen in excess of fifty one million dollars for various charity programs including Hurricane Katrina victim's relief and South Africa girls' education.

Throughout her impressive career, Oprah has maintained her integrity and inspired millions of people with her powerful life lessons. Whether you are looking for inspiration in your personal life, professional goals or simply seeking guidance for your journey to personal happiness, the inspirational quotes and life lessons from Oprah can help you towards accomplishing your goals and achieving your dreams.

CHAPTER 1 - Your Start in Life Should Not Stop You

Oprah is a firm believer that your start in life should not stop you from achieving your goals or realizing your dreams. Oprah herself had humble beginnings in life. Her teenage unmarried mother took her to live with her maternal grandmother in rural poverty. Although her grandmother took Oprah to the local church frequently and taught her to read before she was three, she would be hit with a stick if she misbehaved or failed to complete her chores. Local children also bullied her as her family was so poor that she would be forced to wear dresses made from potato sacks.

While Oprah suffered physical and sexual abuse during her childhood, acting out in destructive ways, this did not stop her from receiving a four-year scholarship. Although she credited living with her father who taught her strength and self-reliance, Oprah has never allowed her start in life to limit her potential or prevent her from achieving her goals.

CHAPTER 2- Be Prepared to Work Hard

Oprah also strongly believes that in order to achieve your goals, you need to be prepared to work hard. Oprah began working on local radio when she was still in high school and landed a job as a co-anchor when she was only nineteen. Oprah was the first female black news anchor and the youngest anchor at WLAC-TV in Nashville. While this position was very factual and needed a cold calm demeanor, Oprah continued to work hard and give the role one hundred percent effort. Oprah moved to WJZ-TV in Baltimore to co-anchor the evening news in 1976 and waited a further two years before being recruited to co-host People Are Talking, the WJZ local talk show. It was this talk show that allowed Oprah to fully explore her enjoyment of allowing her empathetic style to put guests at ease and provide the forerunner for her own show.

As Theodore Roosevelt said "nothing is worth having unless it means effort, pain and difficulty". This means that before you make any steps towards achieving your goal, you will need to be prepared to work hard.

CHAPTER 3 - Surround Yourself With Positivity

Oprah has had her share of dark times in her life. From her troubled childhood through to amazingly successful woman, Oprah has shown remarkable dedication and effort to perform this dramatic shift. However, Oprah also believes that surrounding yourself with positivity can help to achieve your goals. According to Oprah, she is continually "working on not letting people with dark energy consume any of my minutes on this earth".

Most people are aware of negative people in their lives, who will continually make us question our dreams and what we are looking to achieve. Oprah believes that "how you spend your time defines who you are". This means that if you are spending your time surrounded by dark energy consuming negativity, you are likely to struggle to make positive changes in your life. Negativity can be contagious and it is only by surrounding yourself with positivity can you break free of negative patterns of behavior.

CHAPTER 4 - Tomorrow is Filled With Possibilities

Even during the most challenging of days, it is important to remember that tomorrow is filled with possibilities. Oprah has said that she wants "every day to be a fresh start on expanding what is possible". She appreciates that a desensitized "shut down life" is not what she wants from life and would rather work towards achieving that fresh start.

Oprah sees fresh starts as an important topic, with each day bringing "a chance to start over". Since most people spend their time thinking that they are in too deep or have been traveling in the wrong direction for far too long. Oprah insists that this is not the case and showcases this potential by continually striving for new possibilities. Although she has no financial need to continue working, Oprah is continually taking new opportunities, changing herself for the better. While the mind may make it seem like change is impossible, there is nothing in your past, which limits your potential for changing today. Put your thoughts into action and start the harnessing the possibilities now.

CHAPTER 5 - Listen to Your Inner Voice

Oprah is also a strong believer that you should listen to your inner voice. While we all have an internal monologue debating the decisions we make, many of us bow to peer pressure and fail to listen to ourselves. Oprah has been quoted as saying that the reason she still had a show was that she listened to her inner voice "against the advice of many". She believes that had she failed to listen to her inner voice, she and her show would have vanished into a "void of defunct broadcasting".

When Oprah was working as a news co-anchor, she understood that it was the right direction and the right field for her goal, but it wasn't what she actually wanted. When she was offered the opportunity of a talk show, she stuck to what she felt was important and didn't focus on ratings. The people around Oprah at that time, were skeptical and felt this was a bad career move and advised against this approach. However, while this hurt her show initially, people took note and listened, becoming loyal fans.

Over the years, there have been a great number of talk show hosts and shows, which have come and gone. Oprah listened to her strengths and focused on what she knew was best, creating a new television world, which would last decades. To this day, before making any major decisions, Oprah asks herself "what would you have me do?"

CHAPTER 6 - DON'T BE AFRAID OF FAILURE

One of the main reasons why many people fail to reach their potential is that they are afraid of failure. However, Oprah understands that the reality of life is filled with both ups and downs. Instead of being afraid of failure, it is important to accept that the two function together. Oprah believes that "the worst of times are preparing me for the best".

While no one particularly enjoys the prospect of failure, Oprah believes that "it is not failure if you enjoy the process". Although you should not court failure, it should not prevent you from taking action. Fearing failure can cause procrastination and doubt, stifling your creativity and potential. Oprah believes that what you fear the most actually has no power; it is your fear of this thing, which has the power. It is only "facing the truth that really will set you free".

CHAPTER 7 - Learn From Your Failures

The challenges in life should be considered as preparation for the future, making us stronger and more driven to achieve our goals. To believe that you will suffer no failures in life is naive. However, it is important to recognize the learning potential of failure. Oprah believes that failure can be a constructive way to learn from our mistakes. She says "failure is a signpost to turn you in another direction". Failure is an opportunity to re-examine what you were thinking and re-evaluate your plan to move forward. Rather than dwelling on failure and allowing it to bring down your mood or enthusiasm, Oprah advises to "turn your wounds into wisdom", creating a more positive experience for any failures or negatives.

While it if you are in the midst of a failure, it can be disheartening; Oprah reassures us that failure often is hand in hand with making progress. According to Oprah, "getting to what feels right often comes from things going wrong". History is filled with stories of amazing success and progress resulting from failure and adjusting an approach. Thomas Edison made 10,000 attempts at the light bulb before success. Remember that failure is a part of life; the important thing is to get back on the horse and learn from your failures.

CHAPTER 8 - You Reap What You Sow

Another important Oprah lesson is that you reap what you sow. Oprah has a defining creed that "what you put out comes back all the time, no matter what". This theory of "what goes around comes around" is a popular mantra, but Oprah believes that in every level of life, from romance through to work-life, what you are putting out will come back. The main thing to consider is whether it comes back to bite you in the behind. Oprah tries to be fair and respectful, regardless of who she is dealing with. This was highlighted in her show, where she refused to demean her guests by resorting to trashy television. For this reason, the Oprah Winfrey Show managed to sensitively deal with myriad of situations and stories from the prejudices facing interracial couples through to infidelity, "home alone" parents to rape victims confronting attackers. Each topic has been dealt with in a respectful manner, important to Oprah.

This is great advice to follow for every aspect of your life. So, remember that next time you are tempted to be short tempered with a delivery guy or snap at a colleague, according to Oprah it will come back to you. Try to project a more positive outlook and friendly attitude; you may be pleasantly surprised at what comes back.

CHAPTER 9 - DEFINE YOUR OWN LIFE

Oprah also strongly believes in empowerment. She insists "you define your own life". This is an important aspect of building self-esteem and when you "don't let other people write your script", you can gain control over your life. This attitude is apparent when you consider that Oprah had her own ideas of where she wanted her career to go. While others would have settled for being an anchor and following the advice of others, Oprah had her dreams and took the responsibility to put them into action. While Oprah does recognize that it is important to accept wisdom and advice from other people, you should remain totally responsible for your own dreams and goals. You are the only person who knows what you want, need or are capable of. Only you can take the action needed to accomplish your goals. After all, if you don't take the responsibility to define your own life and dreams, who else will?

CHAPTER 10 - Only You Give the Past Power

Oprah has suffered through her share of personal tragedy and throughout the twenty-five years, she met with countless victims of violence, abuse and tragedy. However, Oprah believes that the impact these events have on your life is down to you. She says "whatever someone did to you in the past, has no power over your present. Only you give it power".

We all carry physical and emotional scars, which can be difficult to erase. While it can be easy to slip into allowing the anger and hurt, it can remove the desire to forgive. However, this can be an obstruction in your path to moving forward with your life. Although you don't need to forgive every single person who has ever hurt you, or pretend that your past didn't happen, you should not let this be a factor in your present or future. Only you allow the negativity of other people to play a role in your life. When you accept that bad things have happened and strip these negative memories, you can be free to move on to something better.

CHAPTER 11 - Worrying is Wasted Energy

We have all experienced times of worry. Whether you are concerned about paying the bills, your job, your body, relationships, the past or the future, Oprah insists that worrying is simply wasted energy and time. She believes that it can be a far more positive experience to "use the same energy for doing something about whatever worries you".

Worrying can be crushing to your morale and health. When you allow yourself to become overwhelmed by worries, there is no energy or space left for anything else. However, if you direct this energy and time into something more productive, you will be amazed at what you can accomplish. This can provide you with amazing confidence in your capabilities, boosting your self-esteem and allowing you to solve problems. This "can do" attitude will allow you to banish your worries, fix your problems and move on with your life. It is important to understand how you are wasting energy and prevent negative thinking from being a roadblock. Instead consider the many ways to get around it.

CHAPTER 12 - Become What You Believe

The power of positive thinking has amazing potential. Oprah believes that "you become what you believe" and "what you believe has more power than what you dream, wish or hope for". It is important to have conviction in what you believe and recognize that you deserve your dreams. Beliefs influence every single thought we have and if you believe you are not allowed your dreams, every path you take on your journey will feel like a misstep. This negativity can allow you to see "signs" that problems are a message that you are on the wrong path and should give up. However, if you believe that you have the capability to overcome problems and deserve your desires, you will find a power throughout your journey. This can give you confidence in the good times and strength in the hard times to continue on your path.

CHAPTER 13 - Culminate True Friendships

Oprah also believes in the importance of culminating true friendships. Throughout her amazing career and personal journey, she has found that wealth and fame are not friends. She has experienced that "lots of people want to ride with you in the limo". However, a measure of true friendship is finding "someone who will take the bus with you when the limo breaks down".

Fair weather friends will be there to help you celebrate the good times, but nowhere to be found in the bad times. While a fun friend who knows how to party can fill a role at times, it is important to culminate true friendships with people who can support and love you long term.

Finding and cultivating true friendships is not always easy. No body's perfect, but there should always be a willingness to make an effort and grow. When someone is not being a good friend, it is natural to forgive. However, Oprah believes that "if friends disappoint you over and over" this is "in large part your own fault". While this may seem harsh, Oprah says, "once someone has shown a tendency to be self-centered, you need to recognize that and take care of yourself". It is important to understand that "people aren't going to change simply because you want them to". You need to have confidence in your relationships and know that the people around you can be a source of strength rather than being a liability. You need to ask yourself about the energy contained in your relationship and if "they promote joy" or "are burdensome".

CHAPTER 14 - KEEP CHASING YOUR DREAMS

Oprah believes that persistence is one of the major keys to happiness. It is important to understand that the road to your success may be long. Oprah says, "you can have it all. You just can't have it all at once". Even massively successful Oprah has found that she has had a push-pull fight to achieve her goals. It is important to recognize that what works today, may not work tomorrow, but this is no reason to stop chasing your dreams. You may need to make compromises or exchanges but providing you keep chasing your dreams, you can continue to feel fulfilled. Once you have decided what you want to achieve, you are the only thing stopping yourself. If you allow temporary setbacks and negative experiences to stop you chasing your dreams, you will struggle to find happiness and fulfillment.

CHAPTER 15 - Love is the Key to Real Happiness

While many of us feel that money makes the world go around, Oprah insists that love is the key to real happiness. She spends a great deal of her time sharing with the people around her. The most popular part of the Oprah Winfrey Show was the moments where Oprah shared the "ahh" moments with viewers. Oprah believes that "the happiness you feel is in direct proportion to the love you give". She finds strength in the task of not only bettering herself, but also doing this with others. Simply watching one episode of the show will allow you to see that the love Oprah puts into her work would result in a positive response. Oprah takes joy and fulfillment in seeing others be inspired. Selfish, calculated goals will not produce true happiness. Real happiness is only accomplished with you put your heart into it.

CHAPTER 16 - Don't Follow the Pack

Oprah has always been a leader, willing to stand alone to achieve her goals. She believes that following the pack is a mistake that can prevent you from realizing your dreams. She has said that "often we don't even realize who we're meant to be" simply because "we're so busy trying to live out someone else's ideas" However, "other people and their opinions hold no power in defining our destiny".

Oprah insists, "if you make a choice that goes against what everyone else thinks, the world will not fall apart". While going against the majority may be difficult and scary, it can be important to your personal destiny. Going against the pack means that you will be asked tough questions and you may question yourself about whether you should not just follow the easier and safer rules of the game. However, taking a chance and going in another direction could be vital to your mental health. Whether you succeed or fail, the world keeps turning, but only by challenging the status quo can the world get better. While your small decisions may not feel like a revolution, it is still your decision. It is important to realize that breaking the rules will not break the world. A "mistake" will not ruin your life, but it could lead you down a different path using different knowledge.

CHAPTER 17 - Have Confidence in Your Instincts

Oprah also strongly believes in having confidence in your instincts. She insists that you need to "trust your instincts. Intuition doesn't lie". We have all met someone or been in a situation that didn't feel right. Many times we ignore this instinct but how many times has it proven correct in the long run. People lie, even when they are lying to themselves. The brain filters everything we say and hear but instincts can't lie. Our instincts were developed for our protection and often our gut may know something that the brain hasn't figured out yet.

This instinct can be tricky when it comes to dealing with people. We have all heard the adage, of "don't judge a book by its cover" but it can be difficult to determine whether the person you meet will become a part of your life. According to Oprah, your gut reaction can be assisted by what people show you. However, she warns that "when people show you who they are" you should "believe them, the first time". This means that you listen to your gut and if you have been lied to or deceived once; it is likely to happen again. Don't ignore your instincts 100 times to realize that you have already seen who someone is.

CHAPTER 18 - LEARN TO LOVE YOURSELF

In the modern world of billboards, magazines and movies filled with beautiful people, it can be very easy to be overly critical of oneself. However, Oprah believes that it is important to learn to love oneself. It is only by accomplishing this task can you "learn to extend that love to others in every encounter". A lack of self-love makes it impossible to completely love others. Without self-love, loving others is often a band-aid to cover your own pain.

Oprah has had a public battle with weight loss and weight gain, but it is only by learning to love herself, has she achieved balance. This lesson to loving herself has meant that Oprah no longer has the goal of being thin. She has recognized that she needs to be strong, fit and healthy. Oprah's new body goal is to "learn to embrace this body and be grateful every day for what it has given me".

Oprah believes that an important aspect of learning to love oneself is balance. It can be very easy to give everything to your work, family and friends. However, even super busy Oprah schedules time to do nothing. She believes this gives you time to reflect on the rest of the day and avoid disorderly chaos. If you don't have time to stop and think, how can you expect to be grounded and productive? Oprah pencils her time to do nothing between breakfast and her morning exercise. This allows her to find her grounding and determine exactly what she wants to accomplish that day.

CHAPTER 19 - Love Should Feel Good

Oprah has had her share of negative relationships in her life. However, she has learned that "love doesn't hurt. It feels really good". Oprah acknowledges that relationships can be difficult but this doesn't mean that they should cause you pain. She has explored the problems of low self-respect and esteem and the impact it can have on relationships. When you have been raised in a situation, which did not build your self-esteem, often people find themselves believing that they deserve the pain being inflicted. Oprah advises that if you are in love and it hurts physically or mentally, this is not a good place. This is not normal and you do not deserve it.

Oprah strongly believes "people that love you don't treat you badly". This can apply to all types of relationships but it was highlighted on a Life class section on abuse featured on the Oprah Winfrey Show. In this segment, successful tycoon and star Oprah discussed her past relationships and admitted that she had spent time "looking for love in all the wrong places". This journey was an attempt for Oprah to find validation. She found herself drawing lines when she was assaulted with a door. She reasoned to herself that a door wasn't a fist, so it wasn't the same as "proper" physical abuse. However, when she fell and saw herself in the mirror, she saw that while she wasn't physically battered yet, she was already emotional beaten. This gave her a moment of clarity, where she saw the potential for this to snowball into a far worse situation. Although painful to admit, Oprah shared this memory to illustrate that people who really love you, don't treat you badly.

CHAPTER 20 - Take Stock of Your Life

Oprah also advises taking stock of your life. By this she means not considering what's trending right now, but "the real deal" and determine "whose life did you touch? Who did you love, and who loved you back?" Oprah understands that people are constantly checking to see how they measure up but buying expensive clothes, posh cars and fancy food is not a measure of what we will remember. Oprah believes that "the wonders we're capable of have nothing to do with the measurement of mankind." The "real deal" allows you to make a difference in your life today and in years to come.

According to Oprah, keeping up with others is often a lifelong challenge. Many people find themselves aspiring for expensive cars, designer clothing and other material possessions not simply because they appreciate these items, but to show others that they can compete. However, these things will not make a difference fifty years from now and at the end of your life, you are not likely to regret not buying something. Taking stock of your life is not merely a check of your assets, it is about assessing where you are and whether you are working towards your goals and making a difference in the lives of others.

CHAPTER 21 - Turn Your Passion Into A Profession

When we are children, we often daydream about what we will be when we grow up. Often as adults we settle for a safer option and find that our profession is actually dragging us down. However, to achieve happiness you should consider that a profession is not simply something to make money. While money is essential for basic survival, it is important to remember that your goal should not be to fit into the mold of your role. Aspiring for financial gain is likely to lead you from the path of happiness. According to Oprah, it is only by letting "passion drive your profession" will you find joy in the process of work. This will make you a better co-worker, employee or employer. Deep passion will not dissipate, so it can fuel creativity and fulfillment. If you can find a way to get paid doing something you love, "every paycheck will be a bonus". Oprah believes that if you find a job that you love, you will find that you never actually feel like you a working. Consider that providing you can afford the basics, avoiding stress and anger is priceless. If you are counting down the minutes until the workday ends, you are unlikely to find job satisfaction. While finding a true passion can be challenging, Oprah insists that once you find this, it will feel like natural and "true passion should feel like breathing". Oprah has found that she derives so much joy from her work that she cannot slow down or miss an interview. Even if her days are packed, she feels energized and fulfilled from her work.

CHAPTER 22 - Take Responsibility For Your Own Life

Oprah also believes that one of the most important aspects of finding happiness and fulfillment is to take responsibility for your own life. She insists, "only you have the power to move your life forward". She has said that you are wasting your time "waiting on somebody to save you, fix you or to even help you".

Oprah learned at an early age that she was responsible for her own life. She credits this knowledge with being more spiritually conscious to determine what "we are all responsible for ourselves". Oprah believes that this enables anyone to "create your own reality by the way you think and therefore act".

While in the modern blame culture this attitude is not popular, Oprah strongly believes in empowerment and it is only by accepting responsibility for your own life can this be accomplished. Waiting around for someone to make your life how you would like it is ultimately unfulfilled. After all, your life and your dreams are your own, so you should have the responsibility to shape them how you would like.

CHAPTER 23 - Assess Your Doubts

For many people, doubts and fear prevents them from taking action. However, Oprah believes that doubt can be a useful tool. She has said that "doubt means don't" you should consider that your doubts may be telling you "don't move, don't answer, don't rush forward". While this may be seen as procrastination, Oprah insists that by assessing your doubts you can determine if they have validity. She believes that doubt means that something is not quite right. This could be an internal or external factor but rather than stopping you from taking action, it should simply be an indicator that a few minutes of silence and consideration are needed. Rather than revisiting the calculations or numbers, Oprah suggests allowing you intuition to speak. You need to honestly assess your emotions, feelings and thoughts to determine the answer to where your doubts are coming from. If they are coming from a fear of failure, you can move forward, but if something is just off you are warning yourself against your current path.

CHAPTER 24 - Learn Balance

In this hectic modern world, there are many demands on our time. Many people face the decision of how to spend each precious moment and feel a great deal of guilt when work takes them away from children, loved ones or passions. Developing a balance can be a real challenge, but according to Oprah, "balance lives in the present." She believes that even small decisions should be made according to your drive and instincts rather than spending hours analyzing calculations and data to make your choice. Debating what may or may not happen in the future will cloud your vision and obscure the present moment in a million and one questions. Oprah says, "the surest way to lose your footing is to focus on what dreadful things might happen". While this means that you should not rush headlong into making decision to achieve balance, concentrating only on the future neglects the present. As time passes you will never get back precious moments wasted. When you are next sat at a decision crossroads, it is important to use your instincts to help you achieve both balance and your goals. "Doing the best at this moment puts you in the best place for the next moment". Whether you wish to spend more quality time with your children and loved ones or want to push your career dreams forward, learning to consider this moment will help you to learn balance and realize fulfillment.

CHAPTER 25 - Go With the Flow

While Oprah is a very driven person who embraces structure and routine, she also appreciates that there are times in life when you must simply go with the flow. She has said, "the only way to endure a quake is to adjust your stance. You can't avoid daily tremors. They come with being alive". This means that although your plans may seem to be derailed by events, these daily challenges are a part of life and inescapable. While many of us waste time trying to stop all our problems, whether they are related to emotions, finances or perceptions, it is important to realize that this is impossible. It is a far better idea to understand that difficulties cannot simply be erased and only by standing ready to face what life throws at you can you learn to roll with the punches. Once you embrace being prepared for life's challenges with a flexible response will you find that many of these issues are merely hiccups? If you try to fight off the daily tremors, you are likely to find that they will knock you to the ground. To achieve happiness and satisfaction, you need to learn to go with the flow, finding a way to make challenges work for you rather than trying to control whether they happen or not.

CHAPTER 26 - Evolve

Another aspect of embracing life is to acknowledge that the "point of being alive is to evolve into the complete person, you were intended to be. While many of us find the idea of change a little daunting, people, surroundings and even the world are constantly evolving. It is important to understand that while you may have a little voice inside trying to convince you not to change, there is also a small voice encouraging you to take action. Oprah believes that we can only truly evolve when we "stop long enough to hear the whisper you might have drowned out." This small voice may be "compelling you towards the kind of work you'd be willing to do even if you weren't paid." While you may have taken any old job just to pay the bills, it is important to realize that you may be staying put or taking another job you didn't want simply because of the paycheck. While your small voice is encouraging you to evolve and lead you towards your dream job, it is often drowned out by salary increases, benefit packages and other incentives. Many people find that their career "path" is simply based on taking one job to survive, which snowballs into a career. It is important to recognize if you are on this path and stop to listen to your little voice, deciding if you are doing what you want to do. Forget about what you need or have to do something but rather what you want to do. The small voice leading you to evolve will tell you what path you need to take to achieve fulfillment and happiness.

CHAPTER 27 - Be Honest With Yourself

Happiness can only come from honesty, but while many of us take pride in being honest with others we may be deceiving ourselves. According to Oprah, the only path to happiness is to "stop pretending you're anything other than what you are". Whether you are lying to please others or to protect yourself from being hurt, you cannot be happy by denying what you are inside. Whether you are concerned about whether the people in your life may find aspects of you strange or not even know the real you, this doesn't mean that you should not be honest with yourself and accept who you are.

Many of us have fears about who we really are. Whether you are concerned about whether you fit into the cultural ideology you were raised in or will be accepted by your loved ones, being honest with yourself is the only way to accept yourself. Instead of trying to fit into a particular mold or box by changing yourself, you should realize that happiness only comes from honesty of your inner self.

Oprah has said in interviews, "my own truth and only my own truth could set me free". External acknowledgments such as promotions, awards or marriage cannot offer you freedom and happiness. While these acknowledgments can make you feel good, they are only a reward for playing a role.

The only way to find "salvation" and happiness is to be truthful.

CHAPTER 28 - Excellence Outweighs Prejudice

Oprah has faced a great many challenges and prejudices in her life, but she firmly believes that excellence far outweighs prejudice. This winner of Miss Black Tennessee at the age of eighteen could have easily been dismissed as just a pretty face, but Oprah constantly strove for excellence. Her upbringing prepared Oprah to "believe that excellence is the best deterrent to racism and sexism". She has maintained, "that's how I operate my life". Despite beginning her career at a time when her color and her sex could hold her back, Oprah found that doing her best to excel was the best way to deal with negative or hurtful biases. This was not simply to prove to others that she was good enough, but to follow her own goals.

This spirit was showcased on an episode of the Oprah Winfrey show, when Oprah met with people with Ku Klux Klan and neo-Nazi views and beliefs. When she was verbally attacked, Oprah maintained her professionalism and mature grace. She defended the rights of free speech and tried to move to a more positive perspective. This show received great accolades and she would eventually receive an apology from the guest who insulted her. Rather than stooping to play dirty, by maintaining her excellent standard Oprah showed her true personality and encouraged others to change their minds. This attitude of integrity is often associated with

Oprah who believes that, "real integrity is doing the right thing, knowing no body's going to know whether you did it or not."

CHAPTER 29 - Celebrate Life

Oprah also believes that the key to fulfillment is to celebrate life. "The more you praise and celebrate your life, the more there is in life to celebrate". Many people spend their time chasing their dreams and forgetting to praise and celebrate their accomplishments. This can mean that achieving their goals or accomplishing their dreams means nothing. Oprah believes that embracing a celebration of life every day, allows you to make it part of every aspect of your life. Rosier tinted glasses allow you to see a stronger power in the world, especially when you take the time to stop, look and celebrate. It is only by taking the time to see the great things in your life will you be able to appreciate your accomplishments and be prepared for more.

We all know "Negative Nellies" who never seem to be happy. These types of people never take the time to celebrate occurrences in their life, meaning that they are perpetually unhappy. These types of people wouldn't even celebrate a lottery win, as they would be worrying about tax. If you want to be happy, learn to celebrate life and you will be amazed at the things you will find yourself celebrating as you embrace life and happiness.

CHAPTER 30 - Be Thankful

Another aspect of celebrating life is to be thankful. Many of us have a long list of things we want. These could be things we didn't have in the past or we have seen someone else enjoying but focusing on what we don't have is not going to make us feel any sense of happiness. The only way to find joy in our lives is to appreciate what we do have rather than constantly looking for what we are lacking.

According to Oprah, we should "be thankful for what you have and you'll end up having more". However, "if you concentrate on what you don't have, you will never ever have enough". Whether you want more money, a better car or a bigger family, it is important to be thankful and appreciate what you do have.

CHAPTER 31 - Dream Big

Oprah also encourages others to dream big. She advises that dreams are not simply accomplishments. While traveling or paying off debts may seem important, these things are not life goals. Oprah suggests that you should "dream a bigger dream for yourself". Rather than concentrating only on these accomplishments, you should remember the dreams driving them. Most people don't want money simply to have money, they dream of money for what they can create with it. People don't tend to travel just to get a few holiday snaps; they want the experience of different cultures, sights and sounds.

Oprah has created episodes of The Oprah Winfrey Show, which focused on dreams. In one episode, she asked viewers to let her know their dreams and she organized to have them come true. When the viewers who were dreaming of paying off debt or riding a camel had fulfilled their dream, they found that they had not found their real dream. This meant that once these superficial milestones were completed they had nothing left of their dreams.

Why not embrace the principle behind the Confucius quote. "Shoot for the moon. Even if you miss, you'll land among the stars". This means that if you dream big and fall slightly short, you will still achieve amazing things.

CHAPTER 32 - Keep Climbing

Many people question why Oprah keeps going. She was a beauty queen, successful anchor, award winning talk show host, author, philanthropist and business woman. While many people would be happy achieving even one of these goals, for Oprah it is simply not enough. She believes that when you reach the "peak of a mountain top, you have two choices: you can come down from the mountain" spending the rest of your life thinking about the beauty up there or "create a vision, look upward and see the next mountain" to start climbing again.

While the outside perspective is that Oprah must have achieved all of her dreams and goals years ago, she continues to follow her inner desires. When it appears that she has reached the peak of her career potential such as with her amazingly famous talk show, she simply takes a step back to reexamine life and see the potential for more room to grow. In this case, while others were wondering about what she could possibly do next, Oprah went ahead and started a whole new network. This allowed her to encourage new programs, which would help her to fulfill her dreams in a different way. The point where she reached her goal was not a finish line but the start of new possibilities. Oprah believes that keeping climbing is the never-ending path to following your inner desires. This process of growth will allow you to use your abilities in the best way possible.

CHAPTER 33 - DON'T HOLD ON TOO TIGHT

Many people make the mistake of trying to find happiness and holding on too tight. Oprah believes that hanging on to something will not necessarily make it stay. In fact, if you grip too tight to make it stay, it may actually be better if it goes. This is true of relationships, goals and possessions. In The Oprah Winfrey Show, she has had many episodes, which focused on dysfunctional relationships and has said, "if a man wants you, nothing can keep him away". However, "if he doesn't want you, nothing can make him stay". In a situation where a force of will is determining a relationship, no one wins.

Oprah acknowledges that this can be a scary and challenging prospect. She says, "one of the hardest things in life to learn is which bridges to cross and which to burn". However, if you have found that you are holding on too tight to any aspect of your life, you should stop and consider why you are gripping so tight and whether it is actually creating happiness. Chances are when you assess the situation, you will find that if you feel you need to hang on tight, and this is actually stopping you from achieving happiness.

CHAPTER 34 - JOY IS JOY

Another important step towards happiness and fulfillment is to realize that "the commonality in the human experience is the same". Oprah has spent decades talking to a wide range of people who have different experiences and various worldviews. This love for connecting with people and sharing stories has showcased the human condition and lead Oprah to the belief that "We [all] have the same sorrows and the same triumphs. Joy is joy is joy." Whether we are feeling sadness or hurt it is easy to feel that we are alone. Since life is filled with unique ups and downs, it is easy to assume that no one can fully appreciate what it's like. However, this is not true. We all share the same sorrows, triumphs and joys. From your parents to the girl who served you in the coffee shop, your tax adjuster to the jerk who cut you off this morning on your way to work. It is only by realizing that the human experience of emotion is the same for everyone can you take a new stance on empathy, sympathy and understanding. Oprah has embraced this and treats everyone with respect. Despite being a powerful and successful woman, she has said, "I don't yell at people, I don't mistreat people, I don't talk down to people, so no-one else in this building or vicinity has the right to do it."

CHAPTER 35 - Be Forgiving and Care for Your Body

Oprah has had a very long and public battle with her body image. However, after years of losing and gaining weight, she has learnt that the key to personal happiness is to "be gentle, be forgiving and be generous with yourself" She suggests that "next time you look into a mirror, try to let go of the storyline that says you're too fat, too sallow, too ashy or too old". She advises that, "When the criticism drops away what you will see then is just you, without judgment."

Oprah believes that there is no right or wrong for your body. This means that you need to step away from judging your body and be forgiving of any flaws. When you forgive and begin to care for your body, you will be able to see who you really are and be grateful for the body, which carries you through your life every day. Oprah has said that she finally realized "being grateful to my body was the key to giving more love to myself". Rather than pushing herself with grueling workouts and strict diets, she now considers "healthy food and exercise not as a necessary evil but as a daily practice that gives me life".

Oprah suggests that rather than punishing yourself with a strict diet regimen, you learn that food is good for you and you can feel fit and healthy once you accept the important role it plays in your life. Forgive all of your perceived flaws, which you think only surgery can fix and you may be pleasantly surprised at the more positive outlook you develop on life. Once you learn to love yourself, you will also find it easier to love others and accept love.

CHAPTER 36 - Value the Important Things In Life

While many people consider that money makes the world go around, they fail to appreciate that money alone will not provide happiness. However, Oprah stresses that it is important to value the important things. She says, "when you undervalue what you do, the world will undervalue who you are". She insists that you are only as important as you think you are. You need to have faith in your work and skills rather than focusing on your salary package. This will allow the world to begin to see your true abilities.

Additionally, you should consider the value of all of the important things in your life. Whether you take pride in having an attractive garden, enjoy spending quality time with your children or enjoy giving to others, these things are likely to be a valuable part of your life. While these types of things do not have a financial reward, they are truly priceless.

When you begin to value all of the important things in life, you will find it easier to stick up for yourself and you will no longer equate your esteem with how much or how little you earn each month.

Chapter 37 - Take Risks

Oprah believes that it is important to "stay the course and don't be influenced by outside forces" She has questioned, "What would life be without taking a risk?" and advises that people "stay the course and don't be influenced by outside forces". When Oprah decided to end the run of The Oprah Winfrey Show, there were many people who thought she was mad. The show was still receiving amazing ratings, with plenty of celebrities, personalities and guests willing to come on the show. However, Oprah was ready for new challenges and it was only by taking a risk was she able to establish her own cable channel. Oprah insists that without taking a risk, we will never accomplish any goal. While outside forces will always be there to make the path difficult, risks are needed for success.

While many of us have dreams and goals, you will never accomplish your goals without being prepared to take a risk. Oprah says, "What I know for sure is that if you want to have success, you can't make success your goal". Therefore, you must be ready to take risks and if you do not succeed, you can use the experience to learn from any mistakes.

CHAPTER 38 - SERVE OTHERS

While many of us are concerned about achieving our goals and dreams, Oprah believes that it is important to remember the importance of serving others. Oprah says, "when you shift your focus from success to service, your work as a teacher, clerk or dot comer will instantly have more meaning". Oprah relished the opportunity to share the "ahh" moments with her audience and found this made her accomplishments feel even greater. By sharing her happiness and triumphs with other people that she found her true voice and created real success. Oprah lives by this lesson and she doesn't simply talk, she shares and leads.

Oprah has also recognized that it is by serving others that she has developed a greater sense of joy. She has said, "I've received so much more; the unparalleled joy of watching each of them take flight." Oprah has learned that leading and teaching is very rewarding and established the Oprah Winfrey Leadership Academy. This allowed her to serve and share with the girls, offering her new levels of pride and joy.

CHAPTER 39 - UNDERSTAND OTHERS

Oprah believes that regardless of our gender, nationality or upbringing, all people have one thing in common; we all "want to be validated. We want to be understood." When meeting all types of guests on her show, from superstars, presidents and industry leaders, all people share the same desire of wanting to be understood. This need fuels many of our goals and actions, driving us to reach out to others. Oprah believes that this need is the reason why we ask if we are doing well or if we look good. She says that in order to understand others, we need to take the time to say "I see you, I hear you and what you say matters to me."

Oprah used this to understand the reasons and motivations of all her guests on the show. Regardless of whether the views of the guest meshed with her own personal beliefs, Oprah took the time to understand others. This attitude of respect, empathy and understanding ensured that Oprah maintained her position as the most influential woman on television. She has said that she "talked to nearly 30,000 people" on the Oprah Winfrey Show and "all 30,000 had one thing in common; they all wanted validation". We all seek validation and understanding, in relationships, work or material possessions. However, we all know that validation cannot be obtained from these things.

CHAPTER 40 - EMBRACE SPIRITUAL POWER

The final life lesson from Oprah is that in order to attain success, fulfillment and happiness, it is important to embrace spiritual power. Oprah believes that "there is no real power without spiritual power". Despite Oprah working hard to become one of the most powerful women in America, she attributes much of her success to embracing spiritual power. She says that spiritual power is " a power that comes from the core of who you are and reflects all that you were meant to be."

This means that in order to achieve your goals and dreams, you must be prepared to recognize and embrace your spiritual power. Regardless of whether you have a high-powered career, prosperous dot com or influential position, you will not truly understand real power until you have combined this with your spiritual power.

Your spiritual power will allow you to attain balance and harmony in your life, which will allow you to enjoy your successes and realize your dreams. Although Oprah has strong religious beliefs, she insists that spiritual power and belief is not simply "the bearded guy in the sky". She sees God as a life force. She has said, "I think if you believe in awe and wonder and mystery, then that is what God is". She strongly believes that there is something simply divine about the world and although it is hard to define it is important to understand this divinity all around us and inside us.

CONCLUSION

Regardless of where you are in your life, it can be difficult to realize your goals and dreams. Oprah can provide guidance to assist you in obtaining fulfillment and true happiness. This "Billionaire Every Woman" can provide a true example of the capabilities of what effort and drive can create. It can be very easy to dismiss our failings on our background, personal circumstances or prejudices, but Oprah shows that regardless of these things, you can achieve your goals and reach your dreams. By serving others, knowing yourself and embracing your power, you can enjoy the satisfaction of attaining your goals and dreaming big.

While Oprah may be considered to be a legend, she provides a constant reminder that anyone, regardless of how "ordinary" they are, can achieve their goals and dreams. She encourages us to understand that we deserve our dreams and the only things holding us back are ourselves. We should always try to "do our best" and while this is not likely to earn us a gold star, it will involve failure, success, challenges and triumphs. Doing your best means giving it your all and embracing the journey.

While many people look to "get rich quick" schemes, plans and books, Oprah believes that "whatever your goal, you can get there if you are willing to work". She insists that there is no easy way to accomplish your true potential. Success comes only from passion in your goals and the willingness to work for it, no matter the cost. The important thing is not to be afraid of failing, Oprah insists that rather than worrying about failure and being afraid to try, you should consider that "failure is another steppingstone to greatness". Whatever your dreams, Oprah believes that you should simply hold your standards high and be prepared to work hard. Nobody has the power to stop you and hold you back.

Whether you were seeking help to improve your personal life, boost your career or simply looking for guidance in life, I hope this book was able to help you to embrace the life lessons of Oprah and attain your goals. I wish you every success with implementing these powerful life lessons and hope that you begin to dream big, enjoying success and fulfillment. Regardless of your background, race, gender or beliefs, you deserve your happiness and only you have the power to stop you.

To hear about Entrepreneur Publishing's new books first (and to be notified when there are free promotions), sign up to their New Release Mailing List.

Finally, if you enjoyed this book, please take the time to share your thoughts and post a review on Amazon. It'd be greatly appreciated!

Thank you and good luck!

Preview Of 'Social Media Marketing: 21 Powerful Marketing Tips To Help Skyrocket Traffic, Establish Authority And Build A Media Platform For Your Business" from Entrepreneur Publishing

HOW TO SKYROCKET YOUR ONLINE TRAFFIC

If you are starting your business or even if you have been in business for a while and you are now looking to expand your traffic in order to increase your Return on Investment (ROI). With the growth in technology, you can now be able to market you business to millions and all at no cost. All you need is to know how to navigate the vastness of the web, once you are able to do that there is no limit to the number of people you will get into contact with.

In this book you will be able to learn tips on how to increase your traffic using social media for marketing. The lessons will be divided into three chapters each covering a major section of the message behind the idea of the book.

When going into social media marketing, you first have to establish the niche that you are interested in. It is imperative that you have a specific one so that you are able to focus all your energy and time to achieving the best possible results. Here are the seven tips on how to improve and even skyrocket your websites traffic. You should choose a niche that you want to be well identified with.

1. SPYING ON MARKETING COMPETITORS
It would be a wise move to first scrutinize the marketing strategy that is being used by your competitors on the social media community. When you join the social media community so as to find people to convert into your visitors and hopefully your customers, you will find that your competitors are there too. For a beginner, or even

businessman who has been in the business for some time, this is a blessing in disguise. First study your enemies and potential customers. Study on how your target audience does things online, how they write their posts, things that they like and even what they share, and then try to mimic that. You should also study how your competitors carry out their jobs online and use that to make yourself even more desirable to consumers.

2. BLOG

When you decide to do your marketing on social media, you should know that the content that you post should be of great quality and is very essential. You should start a blog and ensure that whatever you talk of on the social media networks has a hyperlink leading the reader back to your blog where you put more information on the topic. For you to attract and maintain visitors on your blog you need to have great and relevant, but also easy to read and understand content. To ensure that your blog is as effective as it could ever be, follow the points given below:

- **Type of Content**
  When it comes to the type of content on your site, make sure that you have the best, informative and easy to understand information. When you go online to look for information, you are not looking to go and start deciphering anything; you just

want something that you will easily understand and has informing content.

- **Regularity**

  For any blog to be able to attract visitors and keep them coming back having great content doesn't totally help you, you need to be able to at least blog once or twice a week. If you find that you at times go for weeks without blogging, and then know that you will most definitely lose most of your visitors gained through blogging.

- **Target Audience**

  If you have more than one types of content that you want the online visitors to learn about, you can use different accounts for different content. This way you are able to manage and grow each account with the sole purpose of selling a certain single product.

- **The Content**

  Things you should have covered for the content include such a thing as the person who creates it and the ways in which you plan to promote it. It is okay to hire outside help in coming up with the content in case you are not well versed with the topic at hand.

  You should also find some ways such as attaching their hyper links into comments you make on other blogs or even Facebook and Twitter. This will generate some increased visits to your blog, especially if your comment was well written.

3. BUILD A SOCIAL PRESENCE

When you are looking to create your online social presence, you need to first come up with goals and establish your objectives. When you are building a social media marketing account on Facebook, Twitter, Pinterest or even Instagram, you need to follow the following to ensure that you hit the right target that you are aiming at. These are points that your goals should have in order to simplify the process:

- **Specific**
  You need to have goals that are specific and not all rounded; this will enable you to get more and relevant information instead of having information about everything all at the same time.

- **Measurable**
  Your goals should not be such that you are not able to measure them.   When you are able to measure your goals, it makes it easier for you to plan on how to execute them and even able to break it down into small parts so that you are able to measure the far you have gone and the part you are still to work on. This will motivate you while at work, when you see the much you have covered, you get motivated to

complete the remaining parts.

- **Attainable**
  It is okay to be ambitious when setting your goals or even when   working, but you should never make or set goals that you will not be able to achieve. Having big dreams is not a bad thing, it is just more easier to achieve what you are working on if you keep seeing improvements along the way, goals that are not attainable will make you lose hope once you notice that you are not making any development in that front.

- **Relevant**
  As you have already read several times on this book already, finding   the niche that will best express your points and give you the online presence you deserve. Focus on a relevant topic so that you do not end up wasting your time with trying to focus on many ideas at the same time. Relevancy can range from you to the consumer and even the distributor at times. Making the content on your website relevant to all those who visit and your target is a way of getting you repeat visits from the people who visit.

- **Time-bound**

You should come up with ideas that are time bound in the sense that you can easily work on tasks based on certain periods of time. This means that you come up with goals that are achievable in given periods of time. This is a very effective way of keeping yourself and anyone else that you might be working with, motivated.

You should also make sure that the story that you tell in your website, is unique and targeted to a given audience. When you visit a website as a potential customer, you will be attracted to visit that site again based on how interesting and informative you found it. A social media page or a website could be very informative but if the visitor is not comfortable while accessing the information, or it is delivered in such a serious tone, there are very many visitors who will not revisit such a site. Online reading is meant to be fun and easy to understand not super complicated, no one is looking to be amazed buy your jargon of the English language.

4. HOST GOOGLE+ HANGOUTS

When looking to skyrocket you online presence, there are very many things that you can do to achieve this goal, it all depends on what works for you. Hosting hangouts on Google+ goes a very long way in creating you an easy platform for you to demonstrate your products. With one on one chats and group chats, you will end up creating a good relationship with your potential customers. If you are really good at conversing and connecting with people, you will not only have one time customers, but will create a good list of repeat customers.

- **Think about your audience first**
  When you plan on hosting a hangout, make sure you understand the needs and wants of your audience. Make the topics appealing and ensure that your audience has the right to dictate what they want to read and what they don't.

- **End Goals**
  With end goals being specific you will be able to find out the return on investment of each hangout. Having specific goals is a good thing since it motivates you to keep going when you see what you have achieved and what is left to be done.

- **Conversation Angle**
  When you are addressing your readers on your blog, you should make sure to approach topics in a way that stands out from the rest. Make sure that you find a great topic and deliver it accordingly. Focus on the keywords in your conversation and your hangout will be at the top on Google.

- **Practice**
  The only sure way of being good at hosting a Google+ hangout is by practicing. When you are

looking to master something, you need to keep doing it repeatedly in order to understand it and be able to do it without any difficulties in the future. You will be able to learn even where you can have your videos found. This will also help you in continuously improving your show with time.

- **Scheduling Your Hangout**
Now that you have done all the preparations, it is time for you to come up with a date and time for broadcasting your hangout. You can schedule you hangout for a certain future date and have the permanent URLs sent to the people who are to be involved in the hangout.

Click here to check out the rest of Social Media Marketing: 21 Powerful Marketing Tips To Help Skyrocket Traffic, Establish Authority And Build A Media Platform For Your Business on Amazon.

Or go to: http://amzn.to/1IcHivT

MORE BOOKS FOR ENTREPRENEURS

Click here to check out the rest of Entrepreneur Publishing's books on Amazon.

Below you'll find some of my other popular books that are popular on Amazon and Kindle as well. Simply click on the links below to check them out. Alternatively, you can visit my author page on Amazon to see other work done by me.

How Audiobooks Make You Smarter: 7 Little Known Ways Audio Books Can Boost Memory Capacity And Increase Intelligence

How To Write A Book And Publish On Amazon: Make
Money With Amazon Kindle, CreateSpace And Audiobooks

Gardening For Entrepreneurs: Gardening Techniques For
High Yield, High Profit Crops

Speed Reading For Entrepreneurs: Seven Speed Reading
Tactics To Read Faster, Improve Memory And Increase
Profits

Content Marketing Strategies: How Delivering Sensational
Value Can Help You Build A Digital Media Empire

Kindle Publishing For Entrepreneurs: 9 Steps To Producing
Best Selling Amazon Kindle Books And Building Incredible
Passive Income

Video Marketing: How To Produce Viral Films And
Leverage Facebook, YouTube, Instagram And Twitter To
Build A Massive Audience

Social Media Marketing: 21 Powerful Marketing Tips To
Help Skyrocket Traffic, Establish Authority And Build A
Media Platform For Your Business

If the links do not work, for whatever reason, you can simply
search for these titles on the Amazon website to find them.